Cli[illegible]n as Mission

How to Link the Gospel with Safeguarding Creation

Grace Thomas
Diocesan Environment Officer, Diocese of Manchester

Mark Coleman
Retired Priest, Diocese of Manchester

GROVE BOOKS LIMITED
RIDLEY HALL RD CAMBRIDGE CB3 9HU

Contents

Church Mission Society supports the Grove Mission and Evangelism Series
At Church Mission Society, we believe that every Christian is called to join in God's mission, whether that means crossing the street or crossing continents, and we want to set people free to put that call into action.

Acknowledgments
We thank the brave and prophetic climate activists who have inspired us in our own journeys of discipleship.

First Impression May 2021
ISSN 2399-6536
ISBN 978 1 78827 165 3

1 Introduction

> To live out my Christian faith is to follow Jesus. That must include standing alongside the most vulnerable and marginalized on the frontlines of the climate emergency. As faith communities, my prayer is that we might stand together, emissaries of hope and love, calling for God's justice and peace upon this precious world. Now is the time for action.
>
> Archbishop Justin Welby[1]

There has been a growing recognition over the past couple of decades that our climate is changing rapidly. This is having a huge and devastating effect on ecosystems and people's lives and livelihoods and, if it continues at the current rate, the global outcome will be catastrophic. In 2018, the Intergovernmental Panel on Climate Change (IPCC) issued a stark warning to the world—we had twelve years left to address the climate emergency.[2] As we write this, we are aware of the plans for COP26, where global leaders will gather in Glasgow in November 2021 to review their climate commitments.

The last decade has seen major denominations starting to take more definitive steps in recognizing and addressing the climate crisis. In 2011, the Methodist Church committed to reducing its carbon use, stating that 'failure to acknowledge the urgent need for radical cuts in greenhouse gas emissions was "morally irresponsible."'[3] The United Reformed Church adopted a new environmental policy in 2016, calling on the UK government to act to reach net zero emissions 'well before' 2050.[4] In February 2020, the Church of England's General Synod set a net zero carbon target for 2030.[5] It is clear that, in order to have any kind of impact upon the climate crisis, personal action must be accompanied by larger, systemic, societal action. With this in mind, we ask what actions can we take as individuals, churches and communities to address the warming world, where can we start and how does this fit into the mission of the church?

Climate action, as a term, includes action taken to 'green' our local contexts and buildings—reducing pollution and greenhouse gas emissions—and activism which is intended to provoke a wider political response. In September 2020, Christian Climate Action tweeted, '*To all those Christians saying we should be evangelizing rather than taking action. We are called to do both and so much more…*'

One response to this tweet read, '*Mission is one of the things we are called to—the "stewardship of creation" is another.*' This interaction highlighted two assumptions. First, that mission and evangelism were the same, and secondly that, partly as a result of this understanding, creation care was not thought of as mission. About a year ago, Grace (co-author) had a conversation with a church leader who expressed reticence about engaging with green issues, as they were worried about the amount of time and energy that might be diverted away from mission. This was not the first time either of the authors had encountered these arguments and it was one of the main reasons for writing this booklet. Here, we hope to articulate clearly why climate action is mission in its broadest sense, and how individuals and churches can engage meaningfully with it.

2

Climate Action is Mission

This booklet arrives whilst the world is still in the grip of a global pandemic, which has resulted in a huge amount of loss, grief and change. For the church community, whilst many have experienced a digital revolution in terms of their worship, restrictions and temporary building closures have led to financial worries as well as the concern that people may not return in their previous numbers. This comes in the context of declining attendances across all denominations in the UK for a number of years. The missional call to 'go and make disciples' is as relevant now as it ever was (Matt 28.19). If climate action is seen as additional to mission, rather than integral to it, it is understandable that churches may be reluctant to engage. What we want to argue strongly for here is a recognition that climate action *is* mission and participating in creation care is participating in the mission of God.

Bosch, in his seminal work from 30 years ago, opened his exploration into mission by lamenting that churches did not really know what mission was all about.[6] The conversations that we as authors have had regarding climate action and mission seem to suggest that sometimes, even now, mission is defined in narrow terms. The phrase *missio Dei*, referring to the mission of God, is defined as speaking of the 'overflowing of the love of God's being and nature into God's purposeful activity in the world.'[7] Mission is, in essence, not about us going out and saving people but instead God creating and saving the whole world, including humanity,[8] and us participating in the *missio Dei*, both representing God and pointing people to God.[9] Mission can be described as the outward energy of a group of contemporary disciples gathered as church to express the good news of Jesus Christ in word or deed, participating in the ongoing *missio Dei*.[10] The Anglican Communion's Five Marks of Mission incorporate a holistic view of what mission is.[11] We can see the prophetic nature of ministry woven into the marks, alongside the practical actions that Christians are called to take. So, how is it that some people, like the church leader that Grace spoke to, do not see creation care as mission? We explore three possible reasons for this.

Mission, Evangelism and the End Times

> I look upon this world as a wrecked vessel. God has given me a lifeboat and said, 'Moody, save all you can.'

These were the hugely influential words of nineteenth-century American evangelist D L Moody. Ruth Valerio highlights this widely prevalent view—that the world is doomed for destruction and, therefore, our main and urgent calling as Christians is to make more Christians.[12] The separation of this world from the next essentially separates the material from the spiritual and elevates the latter above the former. Hull likens this idea of 'vertical transcendence' away from this world to Jack's beanstalk or Jacob's ladder, where two worlds are created—the earthly one and the superior spiritual one.[13] This dualism, and this understanding of the world being a temporary, less important residence from which we need to escape in a lifeboat pending its destruction is not borne out in Scripture. In Genesis 9, God tells Noah that never again will the Earth be destroyed by divine hands. This promise is worth noting, particularly when set alongside some of the writings of theologian Tom Wright, who argues that the new creation is not a matter of us being taken to a new place, but rather of Jesus coming back to the present world and transforming it afresh.[14] Wright argues that when the day of judgment comes, Scripture does not point to a movement away from Earth to heaven, but, in fact a restoration of this Earth. The new heaven and new Earth as described in the Book of Revelation is not a metaphor for heaven; the emphasis is on a new Earth, restored, renewed, transformed and—perhaps in a sense—resurrected. Part of our calling into the *missio Dei* is to build for the coming of the kingdom here on Earth, to participate in God's active creation. The phrase 'Your will be done, on Earth as it is in heaven' from the Lord's Prayer is set in the present tense—God's will for us to tend to creation is a present reality, an ongoing calling to participate in the *missio Dei*. Christians are called to serve God here in the present as much as we are called to be mindful of the eschaton. In the Book of Revelation lies the reminder that God is continually present and active within creation—'I am making all things new'—and, as God's image bearers, we are called to do the same (Rev 21.1).

Part of our calling into the missio Dei is to participate in God's active creation

Incorporating the Political into Mission

Prophetic activism has its focus on bringing about change in a wider, structural sense. The goals of both Extinction Rebellion (XR) and Christian Climate Action (CCA) are to transform unjust structures that have led to climate inaction and denial. Their campaigns focus on bringing to the attention of the decision makers, namely government and law makers, the truth of the climate crisis and the need for urgent change.

The discourse around church mission planning largely focuses on the surrounding area of the church itself, and how outreach and connections can be forged locally.[15] Churches embark upon practical climate action by looking at their buildings and land, as well as advocating for further practical action through teaching and worship, and seeking to make positive differences locally. This is often combined with supporting global campaigns such as Fair-trade and poverty alleviation, but engagement of more overt political action is less frequent. This may be partly due, for the Church of England at least, to the established status of the institution. Again, it may result partly from the continuing force of the age-old adage that 'religion and politics should not mix,' which still has potency in contemporary society, with a You Gov poll in 2017 suggesting that many adults adhered to this perspective.[16] Then finally there may be a reluctance to be aligned with activism, such as that of XR and CCA, which has at times been controversial.

However, the fourth mark of mission demonstrably relates to engaging on a political level. Writing in a recent Grove booklet, *COVID-19: Environment, Justice and the Future*, Ruth Valerio outlines how Christians and churches need to engage with governments on the issue of the climate emergency and global poverty.[17] Activism and truth-telling, however these are lived out, are crucial parts of this missional call. Interestingly, this perspective is one which is held by a large number of young Christians, providing further incentive to engage with it. In 2020, YouthScape conducted widescale research that revealed that nine out of ten Christian teenagers were concerned about climate change, whilst only one out of ten thought their churches were doing enough.[18] The research found that young Christians thought that climate activism was fundamental to their faith and wanted the church to lead the way.

Nine out of ten Christian teenagers were concerned about climate change

Integrating Climate Action and Mission

Another explanation for why creation care is sometimes set apart from mission may result from the historical formulation of the Five Marks of Mission. The original marks of mission, published in 1984, numbered only four. The fifth mark, pertaining specifically to creation, was added in 1990, in a response to the growing ecological crisis.[19] This raises questions about whether creation care was, and still is, recognized as an integral part of mission in itself—climate emergency or not. The later arrival of the mark, whilst welcome in the sense that it brought the issue of creation sharply into missiological focus, suggests that care for creation is not considered to be implicit in the four previous marks. Has the distinction of a separate mark for creation care, and its position as the last mark, even contributed to an understanding that it is somehow less important than the other marks of mission?

Climate Action and the Whole Mission of God

During a recent North West Eco Church conference, Andy Atkins—CEO of A Rocha (UK)—stated categorically that creation care spoke into all the marks of mission.[20] To talk about creation as a gift from God is to preach the good news and to teach new believers about Scripture and Christian faith. To take practical action, as individuals and churches, to prevent further ecological damage is to respond to the real and present human need with loving service. To speak out against some of the structures contributing to the climate emergency, and to partake in prophetic activism, is to help transform these unjust strictures. And to take climate action in all these forms is to work towards safeguarding the integrity of creation.

Both strands of climate action, practical and prophetic, are missional in a holistic sense. They are faithful ways of working towards the kingdom of God here on Earth. They take seriously the words of Scripture and the actions of the biblical prophets in whose steps we follow. They seek to build the church through prayerful and committed witness.

Christian Approaches to Climate Action

3

Why Christians Should Engage in Climate Action

Having established that climate action is mission, the next step is to explore the theological arguments that underpin, or support, climate action and the different ways in which Christians can, and do, undertake climate action. The foundational principle upon which our Christian response to the climate emergency is built can be found at the beginning of the Bible. In the Genesis 1 account of creation, God blesses humankind before telling them to have 'dominion' over the land, sea and every living creature. This has been interpreted as permission to rule and plunder for our own benefit. Dominion language can all too quickly sound like the language of the colonial empire-builders of the past, yet it is vital that we see this command within the context of the first chapter in Genesis. Just before this 'dominion' call is made, humankind is created in the image of God. We are the image bearers of God and are called to reflect God's character in our lives. Thus, dominion in this context takes a different slant. It is no longer about ruling over creation for our own self-benefit, but instead cherishing it and tending it in the way God would. It is also a reminder that we are made in the image of a communal, trinitarian God, where Father, Son and Holy Spirit live in, as McGrath describes it, 'a community of being.'[21] This reminds us of our calling to live in a way that enables all to flourish in community.

Dominion is about tending creation in the way God would

Often stewardship or dominion language has generated images of human separation from creation and a sense of hierarchy.[22] Yet, we must not forget that *we are part of creation*. Language such as this can also give the impression that we oversee all parts of the created world, yet there are plenty of uninhabited parts of God's creation. In the speeches that God makes in the Book of Job, which Old Testament theologian John Bimson argues express a creation theology 'every bit as vital as that of Genesis 1,' God declares how he sends rain to uninhabited places—a clear indication that the natural world has not been created simply for the benefit of humans (Job 38.26).[23] Creation is not ours, as the psalmist reminds us, but the Earth is, in fact, the Lord's (Psalm 24).

Finally, as noted in the introduction, the climate crisis is already impacting not only the land, the sea and the wildlife, but also our siblings across the world. Humanity is part of creation, created to reflect the community of the Trinity, and Jesus declared that one of the two most important commandments was to love one another, clearly reminding us that caring for creation includes caring for people (Matt 22.37–40).

How Christians can Engage in Climate Action

Climate action, in the context of this book, refers to action that is taken to reduce and mitigate the release of gases known to contribute to global heating, such as carbon dioxide, and to protect and nurture local—and global—biodiversity. Climate action can be practical, taking action to address the impact that one has personally, or which an organization has, upon the climate. Examples of this can include switching to renewable sources of energy, adopting low carbon forms of transport and reducing high-carbon transport use such as flying, switching to a plant-based diet and insulating buildings. Climate action can also be what we have termed 'prophetic activism,' which involves campaigning, protesting and even non-violent direct action (NVDA).

Examples of Practical Climate Action

Over the past two decades, it has been increasingly clear that we urgently need to reduce the amount of carbon dioxide and other greenhouse gases that enter the atmosphere. One term frequently used as a way of measuring this carbon output is the 'carbon footprint.' A carbon footprint is the total amount of greenhouse gases (including carbon dioxide and methane) that is generated by our actions.[24] The average carbon footprint in the UK is between 5.0 and 7.7 tonnes, whereas in many of the poorest countries in sub-Saharan Africa—such as Chad, Niger and the Central African Republic—the average footprint is around 0.1 tonnes per year.[25] Whilst it is not a perfect measurement, knowing your individual carbon footprint or that of your workplace or church can help in terms of measuring impact when undertaking practical climate action. The WWF offers a simple way to measure personal carbon footprints,[26] whilst the Church of England has launched its own Energy Footprint Tool, to enable churches to measure their carbon output and then put into place measures to reduce it.[27]

Research indicates that the most effective ways of reducing your carbon footprint include switching to a plant-based diet, no longer flying, adopting green, low carbon travel options, switching to renewable sources of energy in the home and insulating homes and buildings effectively to reduce heat loss.[28] 'Having one less child' is also cited as a way to reduce a carbon footprint. However, whilst global population growth is a factor in the climate crisis, research has consistently demonstrated that it is the affluent West which contributes the greatest amount to global heating rather than countries in the Global South, where population is growing the fastest.[29]

Practical climate action, therefore, incorporates all actions that we take personally, and that institutions and organizations take, to reduce our carbon footprint. One of many possible ways of approaching practical climate action in church is through the Eco Church scheme. This is facilitated by the environmental charity A Rocha and provides a framework for churches to enable them to take practical climate action. The award gives churches the opportunity to review their eco credentials in five specific areas of church life—worship and teaching; management of church buildings; management of church land; community and global engagement; and lifestyle—giving useful information and advice about how they can improve their rating in each section.[30] Other similar schemes include CAFOD's Live Simply programme,[31] and the EcoCongregation Scotland and EcoCongregation Ireland Initiatives.[32,33]

Climate Action as Prophetic Activism

It is clear that personal or local action to reduce carbon emissions will not, on its own, address the climate emergency effectively. For this to happen, there needs to be structural change. The other form of climate action that we identify relates to what individuals and churches can do to speak to power and influence wider change. We have termed this 'prophetic activism.' The limitations of language inevitably mean that no description of this type of action is without its problems, but we regard such activism as prophetic in the sense that it is rooted in prayer, discernment and a sense of calling that compels individuals or churches who undertake it to speak out and challenge actions which do not reflect the way of God. Such action seeks to be a witness and to emulate and honour the ways of Jesus and other biblical prophets.

Caroline Harmon, a founding member of Christian Climate Action (CCA), described how the group formed out of the recognition that traditional approaches to campaigning—such as organized marches, letter campaigns and petitions—were not achieving what was needed fast enough. A more proactive approach was urgently required to address this existential threat.[34] Early in their formation, CCA created this statement:

> Christian Climate Action is a community of Christians supporting each other to take meaningful action in the fact of imminent and catastrophic anthropogenic climate change. Inspired by Jesus Christ, and social justice movements of the past, we carry out acts of non-violent direct action to urge those in power to make the change needed.[35]

The group started to take actions such as blocking potential fracking sites, whitewashing the walls of the Department for Energy and Climate Change (as it was called then) and shutting down an open-cast coal mine for a day. In 2018, they joined Extinction Rebellion (XR)—a secular organization with similar NVDA principles. What followed were a number of rebellions conducted in London and across the country, designed to disrupt and bring the issue of the climate emergency into the public and political sphere.

Climate activism, such as that undertaken by CCA, has historical and scriptural precedents. There are examples both in the Old and New Testaments of actions which could be described as NVDA or civil disobedience. In the Book of Exodus, the Hebrew midwives Shiphrah and Puah were tasked by the Pharaoh to kill any baby boys that they delivered (Exod 1.16). They resisted this order, thereby sparing the life of baby Moses. The prophet Daniel also resisted the law through NVDA by continuing to pray to God, rather than King Darius (Daniel 6). When Daniel survived the prescribed punishment of being placed in a lion's den, his actions prompted King Darius to retract the law and to call for his people to instead pray to the God of Daniel. In the New Testament, Jesus refers to actions that could be interpreted as NVDA. Theologian Walter Wink takes the 'turn the other cheek' passage in Matt 5.38 and argues that Jesus is telling his listeners here to resist wrongdoing non-violently.[36] To be hit on the right cheek, Wink suggests, would involve being struck with the back of the right hand—an act, in the context of the time, undertaken by a social superior such as a slave owner to a slave, or a soldier from the occupying Roman army to those that they are occupying. However, to turn your cheek, therefore offering the left cheek, forces the other person to hit you with the front of their right hand, which is something done between equals. Doing this leaves the aggressor in a dilemma. Do they withdraw from their action or continue, but with an action that demonstrates equality between both people?[37]

Jesus refers to actions that could be interpreted as NVDA

Actions undertaken by members of XR and CCA in London Underground stations in October 2019 received widespread criticism. One founding member of CCA reflected upon her decision not to take part, writing about how the membership of CCA is a diverse mix of voices, and decisions made by some may not reflect the opinions of all—'*…we know we aren't going to get everything right. We know we are going to make so many mistakes. We are broken human beings just like everyone. We are not doing this because we think we are perfect for it, but because "If not me, then who? If not now, then when?"*'[38]

It is fair to ask whether causing disruption in this way is something Christians should do. Anglican priest the Rev'd David Baker, writing for *Christianity Today* during the Easter rebellion of 2019, raised concerns about whether causing widespread disruption in protest was consistent with the call to love our neighbour. Whilst caring for creation, of which humanity is a part, clearly fulfils the call to love our neighbour, does this extend even to the point of disrupting people's lives and breaking the law?

In 2019, the now Archbishop of York, Bishop Stephen Cottrell, spoke in a panel discussion at Greenbelt about civil disobedience. During the discussion, he referred to the Sermon on the Mount and pointed out that often, those that we now think of as peacemakers—such as Martin Luther King and Gandhi—were considered to be troublemakers in their time. The early followers of Jesus were also considered to be troublemakers by the ruling authorities. In the Book of Acts, the apostles ignored the orders of the lawmakers not to teach about Jesus and continued to do so even after flogging, in defiance of authorities (Acts 5.17–42). Stephen spoke out defiantly at the council of law and was martyred as a result (Acts 7).

In Romans 13, Paul at first glance seems to suggest that followers of Christ are called to abide by the law of the governing authorities. The word used in Romans 13.1, *hupotasso*, is often translated to mean 'submit' or 'be subject to,' and, crucially, is not the Greek word that would most readily mean obey or conform—*hupokouo*. Throughout his ministry, Paul demonstrated an understanding of the necessity of law and order for peace. He frequently talked about the importance of obeying God's law (see, for example, Rom 2.23; 1 Cor 9.21) but articulated clearly the struggles against the lawmakers and authorities (Eph 6.12). Therefore, it is reasonable to suggest that Paul's words in Romans 13 were not about unquestioningly obeying the law of the land, especially when it went against God's law, but rather, advocating the importance of submitting to, and accepting, the legal consequences of their actions. From a Christian climate activist point of view, this highlights how there can be a moral theological argument for breaking the law if, in doing so, you are adhering to God's higher laws, and if you are willing to accept the consequences of your actions.[39]

Prophetic activism is about voicing truths to power in order to bring about change

In the midst of this debate, often key elements of what we mean by *prophetic* activism can be lost. Prophetic activism is, ultimately, about voicing truths to power in order to bring about change.[40] Jesus talked about the power of the truth during his ministry—'You will know the truth and the truth will set you free' (John 8.32). The philosopher and theologian Charles Taylor talked about social imaginaries—namely the set of values and symbols through which people imagine their social whole.[41] They give meaning to our lives, but this is problematic if the meaning we imagine takes us away from the reality within which we exist. The uncomfortable truth of our reality is that floods, droughts and other severe weather phenomena brought on by global heating are now commonplace. By participating in prophetic activism, we are able to demonstrate with integrity the Christian value of truth-telling.

Whilst the message that has reached the headlines has been about disobedience that may lead to arrest, CCA never insists that anyone has to make themselves vulnerable in this way. Prophetic activism seeks to bring change through direct actions that are rooted in faithful obedience and service to God. Discernment and prayer are central in the decision-making process. This does not easily resolve the conflict that exists among those who agree and disagree with the actions, and some will not be convinced by the scriptural interpretations that activists faithfully lean upon to justify their actions. However, it does give space, and clearly acknowledges, the importance of grounding actions in a faithful response, rather than any other motivator. The central aspect of any prophetic activism is that it tells a truth that needs to be heard, through action.

In this chapter we have highlighted how climate action can be practical, prophetic and active. It is based on the scriptural and theological call to act with faithful responsibility in creation, as image bearers of God, and it arises as a result of the clear scientific evidence of the ecological emergency that this planet faces. What this looks like in practice, is the next question. How exactly can climate action preach the good news, teach and nurture new believers and respond to human need and injustice? Over the past few years both Grace and Mark (co-authors of this book) have, in their ministries, participated in various projects and activities that have sought to live out the mission of God through climate action. In the following chapters, both will describe what they did and how this fitted in with the wider view of mission.

Listening to Context and Calling: Case Study by Mark Coleman

4

My first parish was in an estate in Liverpool, notorious for gangs and shootings. When I arrived in 2002 the church was situated in the middle of an urban wasteland; some houses had been demolished, others were empty and boarded up. There was arson, fly-tipping and much stress and anger. It was a tough place, a nowhere special sort of place. As I looked around and prayed, depressed with the small number of worshippers, I came across people who had a passion for their community. I began to see the world differently as I began to love the place and see the potential.

As I talked about this with congregation members, and people that I encountered in the community, the desire to make things new and renew the landscape for the benefit of residents emerged strongly. We began to dream of growing vegetables and flowers on the wasteland. The vision was blurred, and we were starting from very little, but a calling to serve in a community is to bring hope, to acknowledge that, in Jesus, all things can happen. This felt like an opportunity to bring new life, nurture creation and, through it, reveal something that spoke of God's goodness and the hope of resurrection.

A calling to serve in a community is to bring hope

We applied for, and were successful in getting, small grants to encourage healthy eating, decorate the church hall and do up the church kitchen. Local allotment holders were happy to help with the planting, and the local schools brought children to get stuck in. The small ageing congregation was pleased to be at the centre of the action and began to relearn welcome and overcome fear. This was a time for healing, regeneration and renewing in the community. It was a call to mission for the church, which had been living too long on past glories. Many with no active connections to church became involved. At a deep level there was a shared understanding that this was about new life and the hope of resurrection in a marginalized community. There was less talk about how things used to be. We launched the Chatty Church Cafe which would proudly use the occasional home-grown lettuce in a sandwich. It was a great way to reinvent the church's presence.

When I moved on to my next parish, I was disappointed that there was no scope for a church community garden. I began to listen again to the voices of people in the congregation. The Junior Church leader, who had heard about bug hotels, proposed an environmental audit to see what was living in the churchyard. A passionate supporter of animal welfare convinced me about having a special service for animal Sunday. Some wanted to do a prayer walk so we did one to celebrate Lammastide. It felt like the Holy Spirit was saying 'Let go of your big idea and listen to me.' The church is located at the entrance to a park so when we introduced an annual pet service, we were delighted at the attention from passing dog walkers. I led a series of special communion services reflecting on the bread and wine, 'which earth has given, and human hands have made' and we reflected on God's good creation as the Junior Church made bread in church to bless and share at holy communion. As a church we were learning how in Christ all is connected.

My third parish was in a northern mill town. There were empty shops, rows of damp terraced housing, lots of ugly concrete social housing and patches of unloved wasteland. Congregation numbers had been declining for some time. A local housing charity had set up an Incredible Edibles garden with its clients and there was a multifaith environment action group that coordinated litter picks and tidying unloved alleyways. Instead of setting up something new, it felt much more appropriate to join in with what was already happening—to serve and support, as a Christian and a neighbour. Through conversations with people, I began to see how our church in the middle of a town had a great advantage—we had a recognizable, significant space for meeting in.

On Boxing Day, 2015, the town centre was flooded. Supported by a local interfaith group, Faiths for Change, and the government's Flood Forum, we organized Time for Creation, a conference which brought together those in the town that were doing environmental work. We made a lot of new contacts and people who did not know each other had long conversations at the church. The next year the local field naturalists organized an event with a plethora of organizations planting wildflowers, protecting the moors and running urban clean-ups. In this, our role as church was to be the good host and celebrate all that was good about creation and humans working together to care for it and for each other. This was the church in the public marketplace, enabling the community to care for God's creation.

I see it as part of my Christian discipleship to be active in justice work

It was reading the letter marking the foundation of Extinction Rebellion signed by various climate scientists and Rowan Williams which led me onto the next step in my eco discipleship.[42] I began to feel a growing conviction to participate in actions being taken to highlight the impending climate emergency. I came across Christian Climate Action and felt I had found a spiritual home. I had long seen it as a part of my Christian discipleship to actively love mercy and do justice (Micah 6.8). and began to feel it was time to join in with the rebellion.. I began to feel a sense of conviction to offer myself to support XR and join in the actions being taken to highlight the impending climate emergency. This led to my participating in the rebellions.

In 2019, I headed towards the XR and CCA protests in the centre of London with the aim of offering myself up for arrest, should the moment arise. Sitting in a road, praying with other CCA members, I was asked to move by a police officer. I declined, was arrested and taken to a local police station. There, I sat with other protestors on the floor of the holding area, whilst the police undertook all the administration associated with our arrests. Together, we shared stories, read Scripture, and prayed. It was a time of deep communion.

The response to my participation from congregation and community members has been almost overwhelmingly positive—suggesting that leading with integrity and conviction, even when this includes actions not commonly associated with priestly behaviour—can be a powerful witness. It served to open many conversations with people in the locality from all backgrounds—some Christian, some from other faiths or no faith. I have met many Christians who are exasperated with what they see as inaction in church, and who are feeling very called to give of themselves prayerfully and sacrificially. My activism, alongside the practical action we have taken as a church, has enabled greater engagement with local activism, particularly with XR. I hope that, as a visible Christian presence, both myself individually and the church can continue to act as a witness to the faith and offer an example of prayerful and active discipleship in the ongoing and urgent work of creation care.

5 Listening to Context and Calling: Case Study by Grace Thomas

I currently serve in two parish churches in Moss Side and Whalley Range, in Manchester. When I arrived, it was suggested that one of my roles could be to help both churches become Eco Churches. We started with the 'worship and teaching' section of the Eco Church programme and implemented this by introducing prayers for creation, mentioning the climate emergency in sermons and finding songs that reflected the glory of creation. We soon noticed that congregation members were incorporating aspects of creation care into what they were doing. Articles for the newsletter about green issues began to be submitted and prayers for the environment became a regular feature of the intercessions. Ideas about how to reduce waste and increase recycling started to be put forward. Having built creation care into the foundation of our prayer and worship, it rapidly became the natural language of both churches.

In the local area, I noticed two things. First, there was a lot of interest in initiatives designed to improve the environment, from the 'Friends' of the local park, to residents attending council meetings expressing interest in developing community gardens and increasing recycling. Secondly, I noticed that people often did not recognize either of the buildings as churches—both are small, modern brick buildings that bore no outward features of a church, and people regularly passed by them without registering their presence.

A new group, the Whalley Range Climate Action Group (WRCAG), formed and, having seen it advertised on Facebook, I attended its inaugural meeting. There, I met activists and members of XR, parents of young children and people meeting who had lived in the area all their lives. Two people told me that they were atheists but were pleased that the local churches were interested in supporting. We began to plan what actions we could take regarding traffic, the use of pesticides in the area, the connection with local schools and the overall reduction of the carbon output of the area. It became apparent that I was starting to be referred to as the local 'eco chaplain'—a title I had not devised myself, but one which was assigned to me by a local campaigner.

Without consciously intending to, I was already starting to address one of the other categories of the Eco Church criteria—the community and global engagement—and by sharing news of what was happening in the locality, in our church newsletters and notices, congregation members began to get involved. I recognized that the role of the churches was not to start something new, but to find ways to work with what was already happening. One way in which we thought this could be done particularly effectively was by hosting an event in one of the buildings that brought together all the different groups and individuals so that further sharing, collaboration and action could emerge.

Our first EcoFest was held in 2019. A programme of talks took place—some with Christian themes, some led by members from local organizations—and space was given to all local organizations to showcase their work. The nearby bike hive offered free bike services, whilst a local ethical coffee cooperative held a stall on the green at the front. People of all ages, backgrounds and perspectives came into the building during the day. Connections were made with church that lasted beyond the day itself. The bike hive runs regular bike sessions on the grounds of both churches, and the local XR group, who were starting a samba band, asked if they could rehearse in one of our buildings. Our relationships with local councillors were strengthened, which resulted in the first Moss Side public climate emergency meeting being held in our church six months later. This meeting was attended by congregation members, children and teachers from local schools, younger people and youth workers, students and residents of all ages and backgrounds.[43] In 2020, we were unable to run the EcoFest in the same way, so we went digital and streamed interviews and workshops via our YouTube channel throughout a day in autumn.[44] All of this has led to a much stronger recognition and awareness of both churches in the wider area.

Connections were made with church that lasted beyond the day itself

In the summer of 2019, CCA were looking for a church that would be willing to host a training event and we agreed to accommodate this. Several congregation members attended, alongside about seventy Christians from around the North West—some committed activists, some exploring what climate activism meant for them. Many went straight from this to the Northern Rebellion, which was an XR protest that blocked a main road in Manchester at the same time. I also attended, my clerical collar catching the eye of some of the other protesters, and I had a number of conversations with them about how I felt compelled by faith to be there. A couple of the organizers told me how good it was to see a member of the clergy with them, and some expressed sadness that there were not more.

Following the CCA meeting and the climate emergency meeting, I have had several conversations with congregation members about activism. Some suggested that doing something locally would bring wider attention to the problem of traffic and air pollution levels in the area, which are regularly dangerously high. We have talked about staging a roadside protest, in collaboration with other local groups, to bring the problem to greater attention.

The advent of the pandemic has halted plans for the moment, but there has been a growing recognition that activism such as this has a place within the church. We will continue to pray about this and see where the Spirit leads us.

Through the practical action and the wider activism of the church, and myself personally, many relationships have been formed. One member of the WRCAG told me recently that the partnership with St Edmunds church had helped her to reflect about the place of faith in life. When one of the members, who had introduced herself as an atheist to me, went to London for an XR rebellion, I texted her to tell her that I would pray for her. I was nervous about how this would be received but within minutes her reply came back, thanking me and saying how heartened she had been by both the support of our church and the support of churches in London.

In the last two years, we have welcomed a few new regular worshippers and three have said, at one time or another, that our commitment to creation care was something that had attracted them, or was an aspect of the church that they valued. From a missional perspective, the acknowledgment of our responsibilities to care for the world in which we live has been embedded into the everyday outworkings of the church. The question about the environmental impact of a certain action or activity is always asked. We do, of course, still get things wrong and have a long way to go in our Eco Church journey. Whilst our journey has not led to a huge revitalization of the local church, it has forged links, increased community connections, and has been a reason for a few new people attending. Mindful of Sam Wells' imagery of 'with-ness,' this model of the church stepping out and meeting people where they are is a contextual missional model.[45] Many of the people in the area that I serve expressed a vocal and active passion for the environment and this was, therefore, a place where we could meet and connect. Transformation in the gospels often came through the everyday engagements of eating, drinking and of being with—and embodying this leads to conversations, where the hope of the resurrection and of all things renewed can be spoken. The energy and passion that has grown in so many people, and the way in which this has flowed out in a number of different directions is an encouragement that the Holy Spirit is with us and, through her, we have been able to serve the *missio Dei* in new and exciting ways.

6

What Next?

How can Local Churches Pursue Climate Action as Mission?

The stories that we have told in the last two chapters give a glimpse into what can be done—and is already being done—by Christians and churches. In a faith that has the incarnation at the centre, listening to our contexts is an essential first step in mission. God made flesh in Jesus is to be encountered on the streets, not simply from a distant pulpit. Contextual theology is, as Bevans notes, at the very centre of what it means to do theology today—'We can only speak about a theology that makes sense at a certain place and in a certain time.'[46]

The view of mission as 'find what God is doing and join in' resonates with our approach and understanding of a God who is actively working in creation.[47] The projects we helped to begin, or simply joined in with, all originated in the grass roots, following a process of looking and listening. In Mark's case, through action and service, hope and new life were once again realized in places that had felt desolate. In Grace's case, the church buildings became an important central hub for the many different activities already taking place in the neighbourhood through which relationships and strong, sustainable links with the church emerged. By engaging in climate action and activism in the different contexts, we have both seen how Christians and the local church can be a visible, serving presence in the community, and a place from which good news has emerged.

By engaging in climate action, the church can be a place from which good news emerges

It is vital that all churches actively engage with climate action as a missional calling. There are many ways that this can be done. Below are a few tips that we have found helpful. They are by no means the only ways to approach climate action, but they may serve to be helpful starting points.

Build a Team

Any kind of climate action will be more sustainable if it is planned and supported by a group of people who share similar passions. You may already know some people in church who have shown an interest in eco issues. Ask around, put a notice in the news-sheet, and have conversations with congregation members to help develop a small group. Do not forget to include young people in planning and ideas—as the YouthScape research demonstrates, many young Christians are deeply passionate about climate action and want the church to do more. Ensure that this is a group that includes, where possible, people in leadership roles and people in the wider congregation.

Engage with an Eco Church/ Eco Congregation/Live Simply Programme

Whilst this is not essential, if your church is new to developing an eco-strategy, planning where and how to start can feel a bit daunting. Such programmes provide excellent frameworks, which can help structure your response as a church. They also give opportunities to achieve awards which, whilst clearly not the main aim of climate action, can help to encourage and motivate people.

Bring Climate Action into the Mission Action Plan

Most action plans start with a vision statement and a summary of what the mission of the church is. Ensure that climate action and / or creation care features right from the start. If there is a section about where the church would like to be in a year's time, include a target for a specific Eco Church (or equivalent) award and, in the specific actions planned, use the categories of the Eco Church initiative as prompts for actions and priorities. These might include worship and teaching, buildings, land, community and global engagement and lifestyle. For example, if the church is concerned about 'growing younger,' use the YouthScape research to demonstrate how climate action is an effective way to engage with young people and look to set up a young people's eco worship group that can contribute to planning worship and teaching. This could be developed both in church and in the local church school, if you have one. You could also include a commitment to hold an annual service for creation or commit to growing theologically by offering a yearly creation-related Bible study. For the 'buildings' category, you might begin by measuring the carbon footprint of the church building using a tool such as the Energy Footprint Tool. Subsequently, in your mission action plan, make it a priority to reduce your footprint to an identified level with practical steps listed, such as switching to renewable energy. Using your knowledge of the local area, highlight some specific concerns relating to climate action—such as pollution from traffic, lack of green / active transport networks and lack of green spaces—and set a priority for engaging with named local community groups, leaders and climate activist groups such as CCA to address the issue collaboratively. Embed the idea of climate action throughout your mission action plan.

Explore Ways in Which Your Church and its Members May Develop a Prophetic Voice

There is a strong theological argument to be made for Christians and churches to engage in prophetic action—namely speaking up as people of faith against structural injustices that contribute to the climate crisis. How each person, and each church, does this should be discerned through prayer and conversation—which could happen initially through a newly formed eco group. Issues that people may think it is important to speak up about may be local—as highlighted in the previous point—or national and global issues. For example, people may want to get more involved with the upcoming political events, such as COP26 or local elections, by engaging with politicians, or there may be a collective sense that people want to speak out about disinvesting in fossil fuels—a campaign that Operation Noah has been running for a few years.[48] There is a growing movement of Christian craftivism, founded by Sarah Corbett, which is described as a way of people using thoughtful, crafted works to both 'help themselves and encourage others be the positive change they wish to see in the world,' and this may be an avenue of gentle activism that churches feel comfortable in exploring. Finally, some may feel drawn in faith to participate in NVDA and link with Christian Climate Action. This can be a powerful Christian witness. It is important that people who wish to explore NVDA and acts of civil disobedience have the appropriate information and training. Both CCA and Extinction Rebellion run training sessions for anyone looking to participate in this form of action and we recommend undertaking training and chatting with more experienced people first.

How each person takes action should be discerned through prayer and conversation

Develop Safe Spaces for Grief and Pastoral Support

It is important to recognize that contemplating the impact of the climate emergency can evoke feelings of grief and hopelessness. We need to develop ways to sustain each other, supporting people in our churches (and in the wider community) through their journey of climate grief and eco-anxiety, declaring God's forgiveness and love, and liberating people to embrace hope and take action. There are a few resources available to enable churches to build pastoral care in the climate emergency.[49] One thing that we have found is that providing space where people can simply meet and talk can be very helpful as it enables people to feel like they are not alone and that their feelings are normal. We have held such spaces virtually and in person—informal meetings rooted in prayer and fellowship.

We began this book by quoting Archbishop Justin Welby, who, in a statement in the lead-up to COP26 stated 'Now is the time for action.' It is fair to say that the church has been slow to firmly grasp how creation care is inherently missional in a broad way and therefore act upon this. The urgency of the situation cannot be emphasized too strongly, and Christians and churches now have to act, speak out about the climate emergency, and see climate action as a fundamental missional vocation.

Notes

1 J Welby, 5 May 2021, https://www.archbishopofcanterbury.org/speaking-writing/speeches/archbishop-canterbury-addresses-international-faith-leaders-ahead-cop26 (accessed 23 July 2021).

2 IPCC, 'Special Report: Global Warming of 1.5C,' https://www.ipcc.ch/sr15/ (accessed 23 July 2021).

3 The Methodist Church, 'Methodists commit to carbon reduction pledge,' 4 July 2011, https://www.methodist.org.uk/about-us/news/latest-news/all-news/methodists-commit-to-carbon-reduction-pledge/ (accessed 23 July 2021).

4 The URC, 'Environmental Policy for the United Reformed Church,' May 2019, https://urc.org.uk/images/Children-and-youth/18-25/201905_URC_Environmental_Policy_.pdf (accessed 23 July 2021).

5 CofE, 'General Synod sets 2030 Net Zero carbon target,' 12 February 2020, https://www.churchofengland.org/news-and-media/news-and-statements/general-synod-sets-2030-netzero-carbon-target (accessed 23 July 2021).

6 D Bosch, *Transforming Mission* (New York: Orbis Books, 1991) p 1.

7 P Avis, *A Ministry Shaped by Mission* (London: T and T Clark, 2005) p 5.

8 S Spencer, *SCM Studyguide: Christian Mission* (London: SCM Press, 2007) p 10.

9 D Bosch, *Transforming Mission, op cit,* p 391.

10 J Hull, *Mission-Shaped Church: A Theological Response* (London: SCM Press, 2002) p 210.

11 The Five Marks of Mission are: to proclaim the good news of the kingdom; to teach, baptize and nurture new believers; to respond to human need by loving service; to transform unjust structures of society, to challenge violence of every kind and pursue peace and reconciliation; to strive to safeguard the integrity of creation, and sustain and renew the life of the earth. See: https://www.anglican-communion.org/mission/marks-of-mission.aspx (accessed 23 July 2021).

12 R Valerio, *Just Living* (London: Hodder Faith, 2016) p 98.

13 J Hull, 'Mission shaped and kingdom focussed?' in S Croft (ed), *Mission-shaped Questions: Defining Issues for Today's Church* (London: Church House Publishing, 2008) p 115.

14 See N T Wright, *New Heavens, New Earth: The Biblical Picture of Christian Hope* (Grove Biblical booklet B11) and Tom Wright, *Surprised by Hope* (London: SPCK, 2007).

15 See, for example, M Chew and M Ireland, *How to Do Mission Action Planning* (London: SPCK, 2009).

16 K Burgess, 'Public want religion kept out of politics,' *The Times*, 25 December 2017, https://www.thetimes.co.uk/article/public-want-religion-kept-out-of-politics-t3rk055cx (accessed 23 July 2021).

17 R Valerio, M Hodson, M Hodson and T Howles, *COVID-19: Environment, Justice and the Future* (Grove Ethics booklet E198).

18 Tearfund/Youthscape, 'Burning Down the House', 2021, https://weare.tearfund.org/wp-content/uploads/2021/02/Burning-Down-The-House-Youthscape-and-Tearfund.pdf (accessed 23 July 2021).

19 Anglican Communion, 'History of the Five Marks of Mission,' https://www.anglicancommunion.org/mission/marks-of-mission/history.aspx (accessed 23 July 2021).

20 A Atkins, Keynote speech at North West Eco Church Conference, 24 November 2020.

21 A McGrath, *Christian Theology: An Introduction* (London: Blackwell, third edition, 2001),p 325.

22 Theologian and environmentalist Ruth Valerio writes powerfully about this here: https://ruthvalerio.net/bibletheology/why-we-are-not-stewards-of-the-environment/ (accessed 23 July 2021).

23 J Bimson, *The Book of Job and Environmental Ethics* (Grove Ethics booklet E196).

24 The Nature Conservancy, 'Calculate Your Carbon Footprint,' https://www.nature.org/en-us/get-involved/how-to-help/carbon-footprint-calculator/ (accessed 23 July 2021).

25 Our World in Data, 'Where in the world do people emit the most CO2?,' 4 October 2019, https://ourworldindata.org/per-capita-co2 (accessed 23 July 2021).

26 WWF, 'How big is your environmental footprint?' https://footprint.wwf.org.uk (accessed 23 July 2021).

27 CofE, 'Energy Footprint Tool,' 28 January 2021, https://www.churchofengland.org/about/policy-and-thinking/our-views/environment-and-climate-change/about-our-environment-0 (accessed 23 July 2021).

28 R Harrabin, 'Climate change: Top 10 tips to reduce carbon footprint revealed,' 20 May 2020, https://www.bbc.co.uk/news/science-environment-52719662 (accessed 23 July 2021).

29 G Monbiot, 'Population panic lets rich people off the hook for the climate crisis they are fuelling,' 26 August 2020, https://www.theguardian.com/commentisfree/2020/aug/26/panic-overpopulation-climate-crisis-consumption-environment (accessed 23 July 2021).

30 A Rocha, 'Eco Church,' https://ecochurch.arocha.org.uk/how-eco-church-works/ (accessed 23 July 2021).

31 CAFOD, 'Become a livesimply award community,' https://cafod.org.uk/Campaign/Livesimply-award (accessed 23 July 2021).

32 Eco Congregation Scotland (homepage), https://www.ecocongregationscotland.org/ (accessed 23 July 2021).

33 Eco Congregation Ireland (homepage), https://www.ecocongregationireland.com/ (accessed 23 July 2021).

34 C Harmon, 'The Story of Christian Climate Action' in J Williams, *Time To Act* (London: SPCK, 2020) pp 11–16.

35 *ibid*, pp 12–13.

36 W Wink, *The Powers that Be: Theology for a New Millennium* (New York: Bantam Doubleday Dell, 1998) pp 98–111.

37 We give thanks to Fr Martin Newall who brought this interpretation to our attention at a CCA training event.

38 CCA, 'Reflecting on the train action: moving forwards together,' 19 OCtober 2019, https://christianclimateaction.org/2019/10/19/reflecting-on-the-train-action-moving-forwards-together/ (accessed 23 July 2021).

39 We also acknowledge that climate activism has come under criticism for its lack of diversity. Grace has written more about this here: https://climateemergencymanchester.net/2020/07/28/interview-with-rev-grace-thomas-we-have-a-collective-responsibility-for-our-well-being-and-the-well-being-of-the-planet/ (accessed 23 July 2021).

40 A core demand of both CCA and XR is to tell the truth about the climate crisis and the science behind it.

41 C Taylor, *A Secular Age* (Cambridge, MA: The Belknap Press of Harvard University Press, 2007) p 172.

42 'Facts about our ecological crisis are incontrovertible. We must take action,' Letter in *The Guardian,* 26 October 2018.

43 See one local activist's write up of the meeting here: https://climateemergencymanchester.net/2020/01/22/moss-side-climate-emergency-meeting-a-new-hope-manchester/ (accessed 23 July 2021).

44 Life and Hope, 'EcoFest2020,' 12 September 2020, https://www.youtube.com/playlist?list=PLV6SF16ZUcoafwU5UfEMukMtOglQ5Vtti (accessed 23 July 2021).

45 S Wells, *A Nazareth Manifesto* (London: Wiley Blackwell, 2015).

46 S Bevans, *Models of Contextual Theology* (New York: Orbis Books, 2002) pp 4–5.

47 J V Taylor, *The Go-Between God* (London: SCM Press, 2004).

48 Operation Noah, 'Bright Now: Our Divestment Campaign,' https://operationnoah.org/what-we-do/bright-now-our-divestment-campaign/ (accessed 23 July 2021).

49 For example, https://greenchristian.org.uk (accessed 23 July 2021) has a set of resources and ideas to help people deal with climate grief.